The Surname Mallabar

Susan Morris &
Wendy Bosberry-Scott

ISBN: 1540742539
ISBN-13: 978-1540742537

The question of surnames, their origins, distribution and history, lies at the heart of genealogy as well as being fascinating in its own right.

In the 1980s and 1990s, long before many genealogical sources were even indexed, let alone online, our Surname Report service provided expert assessments of the origins, history and distribution of selected British surnames, using the sources available at the time.

Now, with so many more sources available, we believe that these reports retain their value as studies of individual surnames, and so we are gradually making the Debrett Surname Archive available online and in print for the first time. Some modern indexes have been consulted to refresh and update the reports.

Debrett Ancestry Research Ltd, PO Box 379,
Winchester SO23 9YQ
Tel: 01962 841904
Email: info@debrettancestry.co.uk
Website: www.debrettancestry.co.uk

CONTENTS

Overview

The use of surnames in England began in the Norman period, when surnames were not necessarily hereditary but usually a form of description. Some described the individual's trade or profession; others were nicknames; some gave the father's Christian name; others gave the individual's place of residence or origin.

Different surnames might be used in different documents, or more than one surname given in one document. Early descriptions were fairly elaborate and by the thirteenth and fourteenth centuries these were simpler, but still variable, and indeed the instability of surnames continued until well into the seventeenth century.

Although some Normans would already have had hereditary surnames on their arrival in Britain, the passing on of a surname from generation to generation only became customary in Britain gradually during the course of the thirteenth and fourteenth centuries. At the end of this period most of the population apparently had surnames.

Variations in the spelling of a family's surname continue to be found until the present century. Before this, as most people could not read or write, the parish clerk or other official would write down the name as they heard it.

There are four main groups of surnames:

A - Local names, which describe a person by his place of residence or origin.

B - Occupational names, which describe a person by his trade or profession.

C - Surnames of relationship, which refer to the Christian name of the father or other important relative.

D - Nicknames or sobriquets, coined to describe a person in terms of his appearance or character.

Many surnames have uncertain origins, but the name Mallabar probably falls into the third of these categories.

Origins and Early Examples

Among the standard works on English surnames, the only surname scholar to have hazarded an opinion as to the origins of Mal(l)abar is Ernest Weekley, who in his work *Surnames* (1917) suggests that the name encapsulates the Germanic word for a tribal assembly or council, *Mæthel*, in a compound such as *Mæthelbeorht*, meaning 'noble assembly'. The surname Major is by several authorities said to have a similar origin as *Madalgar* or *Malgar*, meaning 'council spear' and there are very early examples of the latter which support this theory, such as Drogo filius Matelgerii, who appears in the Domesday Book. Thus Weekley's theory is certainly a plausible one, but no medieval examples have been found to support it.

The name Malabert or Malabard is known in modern France and its origins are considered by A Dauzat, editor of the *Larousse dictionnaire de noms et prénoms de france,* to be a Germanic personal name such as *Malaberht or Amalaberht.* This lends further support to Weekley's theory. The name Malabar is thought to have been introduced in India by French settlers.

In the course of this study no examples of the surname have been found in England earlier than the sixteenth century. By this time the name was well established in Newcastle upon Tyne and it has also been found in Derbyshire parish registers from the 1590s:

> John Malaber married Alice Taylor on 13 February 1591 at Croxall, Derbyshire.

3

The Society of Genealogists Documents Collection includes material relating to the Mallabar family of Newcastle and the surrounding district. The name is found in the registers of St Nicholas, Newcastle, from 1588 and in Whickham from 1576. Various pedigrees have been drawn up, including one citing a marriage of a Thomas Mallabar in 1539 at a church dedicated to St Oswald. It is not immediately apparent which St Oswald's this is and as Oswald was a local saint there are likely to have been several (there is for example one in Durham City). The Mallabars of Newcastle are traced back to Mark Mallaburn, glover, whose will was proved in 1590. Other forms of the name noted in Newcastle include Malburn, Mallowborne and Mallabourne but the dominant form seems to be Mallabar.

An obvious conclusion from this lack of medieval evidence, the existence of the name in France, and the appearance of a strong merchant settlement of Mallabars in the sixteenth century, is that the name might have been brought to England by French Protestant refugees in the sixteenth century. An edict was published in 1535 in France ordering the extermination of heretics and this was the impetus of the first of many waves of emigration, although relatively few Huguenots came to England this early; the major influx came after the St Bartholomew massacre of 1572. Although large numbers settled in London, there were scattered settlements in many other parts of England, Scotland and Ireland. Huguenot metal-workers are known to have settled in Newcastle.

However, the name Mallabar has not been found in the indexed works on Huguenots at the Society of

Genealogists, so we have no evidence as to when the name became established in England and this could have predated the Protestant emigrations of the sixteenth century.

Distribution

In 1890 H B Guppy published his *Homes of Family Names in Great Britain*, still the only published work on surname distribution in Britain as a whole. His work was based on printed genealogies and a survey of county directories for the 1880s, in which he looked especially at the names of farmers, reasoning that they were among the most stable groups in society. Guppy found no examples of the name Mallabar, indicating a relatively rare name.

A survey of a cross section of parish registers for the years 1601 and 1602 was carried out in 1910 by F K and S Hitching; incidences of a particular surname are noted by parish and county, although with no indication of numbers of references. There were no entries for the name Mallabar.

A useful guide to the distribution of surnames for the sixteenth, seventeenth and eighteenth centuries in England is provided by the indexes to wills proved, and administrations granted, at the Prerogative Court of (the Archbishop of) Canterbury, in London, which had superior jurisdiction over local ecclesiastical courts where wills were proved until 1858. The PCC thus provides a national index, although it is not a completely representative one, as testators whose wills were proved in the PCC were mostly among the wealthier members of society, and a disproportionate number of them were from the south of England, especially London and

Middlesex. A search of the online indexes for the years 1384 to 1858 found the following entries for Mallabar etc:

1620   William Mallaber, husbandman of Lullington, Derbyshire

1651   Margaret Mallebarr, Shoreditch, Middlesex

1659   William Mallaber, Lullington, Derbyshire

1660   Thomas Mallabar or Mallabarr, clothier of Ely, Cambridgeshire

1691   John Malbar, mariner, HMS Burford, of Stepney Middlesex

1698   Richard Mallaber, gentleman of St James, Clerkenwell, Middlesex

1706   Nicholas Mallabar, of Wilberton within the Isle of Ely, Cambridgeshire

1722   Mary Mallabar, widow of Barton Mills, Suffolk

1726   Francis Mallabar, baker of St Mary Whitechapel, Middlesex

1733   Reverend James Mallabar, clerk of Wilburton, Cambridgeshire

1733   Thomas Mallabar, clerk of Barton Parva, Suffolk

1770   Thomas Mallabar, Middlesex

1773   Hester Mallabar, of Mildenhall, Suffolk

1786   Andrew Mallabar, Middlesex

1806   Mary Mallabar, spinster of St Mary Lambeth, Surrey

1822   Edward Mallabar, gentleman of Uttoxeter, Staffordshire

This indicates a fairly wide distribution, but with the exception of Derbyshire the name is found more in the eastern half of the country. The Newcastle Mallabars, unsurprisingly, do not appear here; it was a long journey from Newcastle to London to prove a will and the Prerogative Court of York may show more examples. The freedom with which the name is spelled is common for this period, especially for a slightly foreign-sounding name.

For the nineteenth century, H B Guppy's survey has been mentioned above. Another important Victorian source is the *Return of Owners of Land* of 1873, sometimes known as the Modern Domesday Book. This source lists, county by county, every owner of an acre of land or more, with their residence (not necessarily the address of their property) and the acreage of their holding.

Return of Owners of Land

Derbyshire	2	Mallaber
Northumberland	1	Malabar

There were only three entries in total for the name Mallabar. In Derbyshire, two men held the name with the spelling of Mallaber; and in Northumberland, one man with spelling Malabar. The metropolitan area was not included in the survey, which probably explains the lack of Middlesex entries.

We turned now to census records. The first decennial census return in England, Scotland and Wales was taken in 1801, but personal information was only recorded from 1841 onwards. From 1851, the age, occupation and birthplace is given for each member of the household, and so these records provide invaluable genealogical information. The latest return currently open to public inspection is that of 1911 and there are now national indexes to the returns from 1841 onwards, although these indexes are not wholly reliable. Census returns for Ireland largely do not survive before 1901.

1841 census
Mallabar (31), Mallaber (14), Mullaber (4), Malaber (1)

1851 census
Mallabar (39), Mallaber (20)

1861 census
Mallabar (38), Mallaber (17)

1871 census
Mallabar (47), Mallaber (19)

1881 census
Mallabar (69), Mallaber (25), Malaber (1)

1891 census
Mallabar (89), Mallaber (32), Malaber (10)

1901 census
Mallabar (84), Mallaber (21), Mullaber (1)

1911 census
Mallabar (142), Mallaber (26), Malaber (1)

The surname Mallabar appears in low numbers until 1911 when it reaches three figures and nearly doubles the number recorded in 1901. In 1901, we have one appearance of Mallabar in Wales. There were no entries at all for the variant Malbar. The variant Mallaber never reaches numbers higher than 32 and the only appearance outside England is again in Wales, but in 1911 when one person was recorded as such. Mullaber appears only in 1841 and 1901 and in such low numbers it is highly likely that these are transcription errors. The same could also be true of the variant Malaber, which appears in single figures in 1841, 1881 and 1911.

After 1858, jurisdiction over probate matters moved from the ancient church courts to a new national authority, the Principal Probate Registry, for which there are annual indexes. An online index for the period 1858 to 1966 is now available and this shows the following references to Mallabar *etc*:

1862	Edward Lowndes Mallabar, Cheshire
1864	John Mallaber, Derbyshire
1875	William Mallaber, Derbyshire
1891	Edwin Mallaber, Derbyshire
1904	Thomas Mallabar, Durham
1912	George Mallabar, Durham
1911	Thomas Mallabar, Durham
1912	William Mallabar, Darlington, Durham
1926	John Mallabar, Durham
1927	Jane Mallabar, Gateshead, Durham
1945	Elijah Nevins Mallabar, Middlesbrough
1950	Beatrice May Mallabar, Middlesbrough
1951	Anne Elizabeth Mallabar, Middlesbrough
1959	William Mallabar, Durham
1932	Gertrude Mallabar, Hertfordshire
1957	Herbert John Mallabar, Hertford
1951	Frances Harriet Mallabar, Kent
1963	John Mallabar, Kent
1964	Arthur Huntley Mallabar, Kent
1899	William Mallaber, Liverpool
1901	John Osborn Mallabar, Liverpool
1862	George Mallaber, Northamptonshire
1944	David Coulson Mallabar, Northumberland

1959   Rachael Mallabar, Northumberland

1898   Daniel Mallaber, Staffordshire
1898   Sarah Ann Mallaber, Staffordshire
1916   William Mallabar, Staffordshire
1938   Annie Harriet Mallabar, Staffordshire
1948   Mary Mallaber, Stafford
1952   Edwin Harry Mallaber, Stafford

1856   John Mallaber, Warwickshire
1859   Richard Mallaber, Warwick
1885   Hannah Mallaber, Coventry
1892   William Mallaber, Birmingham
1895   Elizabeth Mallaber, Coventry
1898   Emily Mallaber, Birmingham
1952   Elizabeth Mallaber, Birmingham
1959   Edwin Mallaber, Birmingham
1959   Walter Mallabar, Birmingham
1964   Alfred Mallaber, Birmingham

1898   Dorothy Hannah Mallabar, Westmorland
1921   Richard George Mallabar, Westmorland
1930   Percy William Mallabar, Westmorland
1941   George Alec Mallabar, Westmorland
1952   Sarah Agnes Mallabar, Westmorland

1924   William Mallabar, Worcester
1959   Gordon Edward Mallaber, Worcester

1876   Hannah Mallabar, Yorkshire
1887   William Mallabar, Yorkshire
1919   Robert Mallabar, Yorkshire
1936   William John Mallabar, Yorkshire
1952   Bessie Ann Mallabar, York

1924   Elizabeth Mallaber, Merionethshire, Wales
1958   John Thomas Mallabar, Down, Ireland

Most of the entries for the surname Mallabar were from the north of England, with a scattering elsewhere in England and a single Northern Irish reference from County Down. The variant Mallaber appeared more frequently in Derbyshire (though not after 1891) and the midlands. There were no entries for the variants Malebar, Malbar or Mullaber.

Printed Genealogies

No references have been found to printed genealogies of Mallabar families.

Heraldry

There is one coat of arms listed in Burke's *General Armory* granted to a Malebar family of Derbyshire:

> **Malebar** (co. Derby; originally from France.) Or, two axes erect endorsed, handles azure blades sable on a chief gules a lion pass. guard of the first.

The note 'originally from France' is interesting. Presumably the Derbyshire family themselves registered a pedigree to this effect with the College of Arms and this lends further weight to the Huguenot theory.

Summary

To conclude, the name Mallabar, etymologically deriving from a Germanic personal name, would seem to have been brought to England from France in the sixteenth century, although earlier incidences in England cannot be ruled out.

Two distinct areas of concentration, probably attributable to just two (or even one) families, have been noted in the Newcastle area and in Derbyshire from the sixteenth to the nineteenth centuries. Other scattered incidences have been found in Middlesex, Suffolk and Cambridge.

In the twentieth century, the form Mallaber appears to have settled in the West Midlands, particularly Birmingham, with Mallabar surviving in County Durham, Yorkshire and Westmorland, and a scattering of instances elsewhere.

Sources Consulted

P H Reaney, *The Origins of English Surnames* (London: Routledge & Kegan Paul, 1967)

P H Reaney & R M Wilson, *A Dictionary of British Surnames* (Oxford: Oxford University Press, 3rd edition, 1995)

P H Reaney, *Dictionary of British Surnames* (London: Routledge & Kegan Paul, 2nd edition, 1976)

P Hanks & F Hodges, *A Dictionary of Surnames* (Oxford University Press, 1988)

M A Lower, *Patronymica Brittanica* (London, 1860)

C W Bardsley, *Dictionary of English and Welsh Surnames* (1901: reprinted, Baltimore: Genealogical Publishing Co, 1967)

C L'Estrange Ewen, *Guide to the Origin of British Surnames* (London: John Gifford, 1938)

H B Guppy, *Homes of Family Names in Great Britain* (London, 1890)

Ernest Weekley, *The Romance of Names* (London: John Murray, 2nd edition, 1917)

Ernest Weekley, *Surnames* (London: John Murray, 1917)

16

George F Black, *The Surnames of Scotland* (New York Public Library, 1946)

Edward McLysaght, *The Surnames of Ireland* (Dublin: Irish University Press, 1977)

T J & Prys Morgan, *Welsh Surnames* (Cardiff: University of Wales Press, 1985)

F K & S Hitching, *References to English Surnames in 1601* (Walton on Thames: Bernau, 1910)

F K & S Hitching, *References to English Surnames in 1602* (Walton on Thames: Bernau, 1911)

Debrett's People of Today (Debrett's Peerage Limited: London, 1996)

The Oxford Dictionary of National Biography (online, 2004–2014)

The Concise Dictionary of National Biography, Part II, 1901–1950, (Oxford, 1961)

Burke's Family Index (London: Burke's Peerage Limited, 1976)

H R Moulton, *Palaeography, Genealogy & Topography* (Sale Catalogue, 1930)

Index to Prerogative Court of Canterbury Wills (The National Archives: online)

G W Marshall, *The Genealogist's Guide* (1903; reprinted, Baltimore: GPC 1973)

17

J B Whitmore, *A Genealogical Guide* (London, 1953)

Charles Bridge, *An Index to Pedigrees* (London, 1867)

Geoffrey B Barrow, *The Genealogist's Guide* (London: Research Publishing Co, 1977)

Sir Bernard Burke, *The General Armory* (London, 1884)

C R Humphrey-Smith, editor, *Burke's General Armory Volume II,* (Tabard Press, 1973)

The Return of Owners of Land (1873)

Eilert Ekwall, *The Concise Oxford Dictionary of English Place-Names* (Oxford: Clarendon Press, 4th edition, 1960)

E G Withycombe, *The Oxford Dictionary of English Christian Names* (Oxford: Clarendon Press, 2nd edition, 1950)

W J Hardy & W Page, *A Calendar to the Feet of Fines for London and Middlesex: Vol 1 Richard I – Richard III (1189– 1485)* (London, 1892)

Richard McKinley, *The Surnames of Oxfordshire* (English Surnames Series III: Leopard's Head Press, 1977)

Richard McKinley, *The Surnames of Sussex* (English Surnames Series V: Leopard's Head Press, 1988)

Richard McKinley, *The Surnames of Lancashire* (English Surnames Series IV: Leopard's Head Press, 1981)

Richard McKinley, *Norfolk and Suffolk Surnames in the Middle Ages* (English Surnames Series II: Phillimore, 1975)

George Redmonds, *Yorkshire West Riding* (English Surnames Series I: Phillimore, 1973)

The Norman People (London, 1874)

Debrett's Heraldry (London, 1933)

J P Brooke-Little, revised, *Boutell's Heraldry* (Frederick Warne: London, 1970)

Indexes to 1841–1911 Census Returns of England and Wales (The National Archives/*Ancestry*)

ScotlandsPeople: Indexes to Old Parish Registers, Testaments, Statutory Registers

Indexes to National Probate Calendar for England and Wales 1858-1966 (Principal Probate Registry/*Ancestry*)

A Dauzat, *Larousse dictionnaire des noms et prénoms de france* (1951)

Society of Genealogists Document Collection

Wagner Collection of Huguenot Society

Rev D Agnew, *Protestant Exiles from France* (1874)

Aliens in London 1523-1625

Samuel Smiles, *Huguenots: their settlements etc* (1889)

The International Genealogical Index (1992): Derbyshire, London and Norfolk

www.ingramcontent.com/pod-product-compliance
Lightning Source LLC
Chambersburg PA
CBHW070254290526
45789CB00004B/1842